ASH and ASH VALE
A Pictorial History

The idyllic scene at Ash Manor, Ash Green, seen from beyond the 13th-century moat. The damage to the west wing was the result of the storm of January 1990.

ASH and ASH VALE
A Pictorial History

Sally Jenkinson

Phillimore

1990

Published by
PHILLIMORE & CO. LTD.
Shopwyke Hall, Chichester, Sussex

ISBN 0 85033 773 9

Printed and bound in Great Britain by
BIDDLES LTD.
Guildford, Surrey

To Kevin, Tommy, Anna and Graeme

List of Illustrations

Acknowledgements

I am grateful to the following for permission to reproduce illustrations and for help with my research: Aldershot Historical and Archaeological Society, Ash Parish Council, the Francis Frith Collection (Nos. 14, 51, 97, 150), the Guildhall Library, Guildford Muniment Room, London Borough of Lambeth Archives Department, Surrey Archaeological Society and Surrey Local Studies Library. Also Mr. & Mrs. M. Armitage, Mrs. D. Blundell, Father C. V. Borelli, Mrs. Britt, Mr. S. F. J. Butler, Mr. T. Childerhouse, Mrs. A. Cobb, Mr. & Mrs. J. Daniels, Mrs. Dubut, Mr. J. Esdaile, Mr. R. Field, Mr. & Mrs. S. Field, Mrs. France, Miss D. Green, Mr. & Mrs. J. Hawes, Mrs. B. Hodgkinson, Reverend H. Jackson, George and Lillian Moore, Mr. & Mrs. O'Grady, Mr. & Mrs. Renton, Mr. Smith, Mr. & Mrs. R. Tolley, Mr. & Mrs. Van Reysen, Mr. Richards, Mrs. White and Mr. A. Woodman.

I would also like to thank all the many local people who have provided information about Ash, and given me so much assistance by recounting their memories. Especially Mrs. Button, Mrs. Caffyn-Parsons, Mrs. Cairns, Mrs. J. Curwell, Mr. J. Knight, Mrs. Knight, Miss Manfield, Mrs. Mapledoram, Mr. & Mrs. Mead, Mr. Mullard, Mrs. Norris, Mr. & Mrs. Saunders, Mrs. Simmons, Mrs. Sleet and Mrs. Tabram.

Advice and encouragement given by Anne Raffermati and John Janaway deserve a special mention, and I would like to thank Joan Divers, Margaret Cann, Carolyn Coltart and my husband Kevin for their help.

At the Ash Tree

In the year 976 Ash was spelt 'Aesc', which meant 'at the ash tree' – an appropriate name, since ash trees still spring up like weeds every year in the middle of the village.

The village of Ash grew up on an area of London Clay, next to the river gravel of the flood plain of the Blackwater River where the soil was good. The parish also included a large expanse of common, part of a wide area of sand and gravel deposited 20,000,000 years ago and known as the Bagshot Sands. Although this land was unsuitable for agriculture, it was important because it provided grazing for the villagers' livestock. The church, St Peter's, stands raised above the village at the top of a small mound of gravel on the London Clay.

The last Saxon to whom the area belonged was called Azor, and he was one of the few Saxon leaders who kept some of their land after the Norman Conquest. When he died he left the land to Chertsey Abbey, and in return the monks said prayers for his soul. When Domesday Book was compiled in 1086, the church was listed and there were ten villagers and six smallholders. Azor's land included the whole parish of Ash and Normandy, but it was referred to as Henlei because that was where Azor would have lived, on the site of the present Henley Park Mansion in Normandy.

In 1537 Chertsey Abbey was dissolved and the Manor of Ash became the property of Henry VIII. A few years after his succession, Edward VI granted it to St Mary's College at Winchester, and the Wardens and Fellows of the College have continued as Lords of the Manor ever since.

In medieval times the most important person in Ash would have lived in the Manor House at Ash Green. A 13th-century coin was once discovered under the foundations, and it is thought that there has been a house on the site from that date. The moat which partly encircles the house would have been a fashionable status symbol in those days. In 1630 Nicholas Stevens leased the 'Scyte of the Manor of Ashe', and the rent was 53s. 4d. of 'good and lawfull money of England'. He also had to 'provide for the Warden and his Officers and servants twice in the year yearlie ... when they shall come to keep court there ... by the space of one daie and two nights good sufficiente and convenient meate drincke and Lodging within the Scyte of the Manor aforesaid. And allsoe good and sufficient hay Litter and provender with stable roome for their horses and geldings'.

The fields which lie between the Manor House and the road to its south used to be 'Ash Green', the road having taken its present course only since 1856. The two ponds on the green are still there. South of the green was a field called Butt Inhams, on part of which there are now four houses of that name. This may have been the site of archery practice in days gone by. Near the Manor House itself is a coppiced yew tree which probably supplied the bows.

Ash Street extended west from the green right through the village, the present Grange Road being part of it. Quite a number of the old buildings along the street still survive, including Ashmead, the *Cannon*, Lavender Cottage, Tudor House, the post office, the

Bricklayers' Arms, Azor Place, the *Greyhound* and Merryworth. Some of those which have now disappeared include the Limes (Lime Crescent), Box Cottage (Sharrocks) and Rosewood Cottages, the Forge, Ivy Cottage and Lickfold's Cottages, all of which were between the *Cannon* and the Forge Works.

There used to be a number of ponds along the street. Most were filled in when horses ceased to be used for transport, but the one next to Church Lane and the one in South Lane remain. The road must have been very muddy until it was made up early this century, even though there were drainage ditches all along the sides – the same ditches which are mentioned in early 16th-century Manor Court records, when Edward Hone was responsible for repairing one of them. In the 19th century many children were absent from the National School whenever it was raining because the roads became impassable.

Green Lane, formerly known as the 'King's Way from Farnham to Guildford', is part of a very old trackway which became used as a drove-way in the 18th century, when cattle and sheep were brought along it on their way from Wales to market in Guildford. Roads often underwent changes of name. White Lane was called Ash Green Way in 1778, whereas in 1443 it had been Farmanyslane, named after William Farman who owned land in Ash in the 14th century. The present Foreman Road was known as recently as 1861 as Paines Lane, named after the Paine family who had lived in the village in the 17th century. The people also used to be familiar with the names of all the fields. One field, north of the present Green Lane West, kept the same name for centuries. Called Hanewyk in the 13th century, it was still known as Hanwicks in 1844.

Although there was once a Saxon church in Ash, it was rebuilt, and the oldest parts of the present St Peter's church are 11th-century. The church has a 15th-century tower, whilst the the south porch dates from the 16th century and the font is 17th-century. Hartshorn was built next to the church in the 14th century as a residence for the priest. It was a timber-framed, open-hall house with service rooms at the west end, and a room with a solar above at the east end. Refreshments would have been served there between morning service and evensong to people who lived in Frimley, who in those days had to travel the four miles to Ash church. There were stables behind the house for their horses. After they had their own chapel, early in the 16th century, they were still required to visit the mother church from time to time, and continued to pay towards its upkeep.

In the 17th century the rector moved to what is now the Old Rectory, and Hartshorn became an inn known as the *White Hart*. In 1685, the innholder was Rowland West and he paid £6 13s. 4d. per annum rent. The pub is supposed to have been used by Jeremiah Abershaw, a highwayman who was hung on Kennington Common in 1795. In the 19th century the house was occupied by the Morris family. Thomas Morris and his wife Mary both died in 1835 and are buried in the churchyard near to the house. The ghost of an amiable woman which is said to haunt the house is thought to be that of Mrs. Morris.

The Old Rectory was surrounded by attractive grounds and approached by the Church Walk. This path was flanked by an avenue of giant elm trees. Along one side there was a ditch, and a large beech tree stood near the bottom. In 1730 the Reverend Harris wrote in the parish register that 'on Michaelmaffe day Three shillings were expended in dreffing ye hedge on both sides & new laying ye Path-way in ye Church Lane'. Between 1711 and 1717 'the parsonage house' was refurbished by the Reverend Edward Dawe, who is buried in the vault under the old chancel of St Peter's church. The cost of the work was carefully recorded in the parish register. This included 'Alterations made in ye Parlour and ye Parlour Chamber, Windows and Chymnyes', and the 'Building of Two New Pantrys'. Five hundred bricks cost 7s. 6d., an iron bolt and two staples for the parlour door cost

8d., and a new lock for 'ye Stair foot door' was 1s. The roof on the west and south sides of the house was retiled. One thousand tiles from Worplesdon cost 10s., 500 laths cost 5s., 2,500 lath nails cost 5s. and 12 ridge tiles were 2s. A new barn floor was made, a new manger in the stable and two stalls for the horses. A new casement window over the brewhouse cost 12s. 6d.

There are two ghost stories associated with the Old Rectory. On Christmas Eve 1884 the new rector, Reverend Walsh, heard a coach and horses pull up at the house. Someone knocked at the door, but when he opened it there was nothing to be seen. The villagers told him that this had happened to previous rectors, and prophesied that it would not happen to him again after a child was born. There is also a story that in 1938 the rector of Ash saw the ghost of a coach and horses drive through the Rectory and on towards the church, with the coachman wearing a scarlet uniform and sounding his horn.

A windmill was built in Ash in 1322 on the orders of the Abbot of Chertsey. It was on Ash Hill, where Windmill Cottages (College Road) are now, and Henrico ate Mulle (Henry at the mill) was listed on the taxation returns for the village of Ash in 1332. The windmill would have overlooked Church Path, which ran through the meadows to the place which became Ash Wharf when the Basingstoke Canal was constructed at the end of the 18th century. From there parishioners would have travelled along the edge of the common towards the northern end of the parish. The strip of good farmland along the Blackwater River would have been meadows, valuable land providing winter feed for the villagers' livestock, and the area which is now Newfield Road was a peat bog where they obtained their fuel. At the end of the parish was Stotfold, later known as Stratford Farm. Now only Stratford Road remains, but the Nash family who lived there in the 19th century are still remembered locally. Church Path was also the route taken by the people of Frimley to Ash church.

Until this century Ash was a rural farming community. Most men were farmers or farm labourers, and the women and children helped too, especially at harvest time. Schools had a four-week break in September called the harvest holiday, which was often extended a week or more because the hop picking was not finished. The children were often absent at other times when they were planting or digging potatoes, picking bilberries or gathering acorns. To store all the produce Ash had many large barns. For example, there was one at Manor Cottage Farm, one next to Hartshorn, one where Walter's Handyman Store is now and one in the middle of the present Manfield School Field. In 1844 a large-scale map was drawn of the whole parish, which had a key listing all the landholders and tenants, names of the fields and houses, and the rent to be paid in lieu of tithes. At that time there were 1,183 acres of arable land, five acres of hops, 611 acres of meadow and pasture, 160 acres of woodland and 2,041 acres of common.

Before maps were readily available the only way to make certain everyone remembered exactly where the boundary of the parish lay was to walk the bounds and this was done on Rogation Day. In 1704 there had been a dispute, and so three large stones were taken from the churchyard to mark the boundary between Ash and Wyke. One of them can still be seen, lying in the corner of the field behind the Scout Headquarters at Harpers Road Recreation Ground.

Another old custom in the village concerned the maintenance of the fence around the churchyard. Responsibility was divided between the various property owners in the parish. For example, in 1781 the fourth and fifth sections on the north side were repaired by Robert Robinson, the farmer at Bricklyn, the 12th by the occupant of Tudor House, George May, and the 18th by Solomon Dayrolle, the owner of Henley Park Mansion.

The east side was maintained by people who lived in Frimley, and the west side by the occupant of Hartshorn.

Besides farming, there were a number of other jobs to do in the village. Robert le Smyth took over a smithy in Ash from his father, William, in 1343. Richard the mason lived in Ash in the 13th century, and John le Carpenter paid 6d. per annum for a rood of land called Mathoueslond in 1347. Richard and Nicholas Heather were carpenters in the early 18th century. Richard was paid 8s. for 'ye new seat' in the chancel of the church in 1709, and £4 1s. for 'twelve seats in the gallery for the singers' in 1729. John Paine was a carpenter in the early 19th century and altered the gallery in the church so that an organ could be installed. John Faggotter was the sawyer who in 1716 made the planks for the new floor of the rector's barn. George Smith was the bricklayer who built the vault under the chancel at St Peter's church in 1709 and did some alterations to the Rectory a few years later. William Nash was a cooper who took an apprentice in 1724, and Benjamin Beazer and William Smallpiece were cordwainers. Richard Cobbett was a clothier in 1606 and Samuel Cork was a blanket weaver in 1815. Domestic pottery was made in Ash from the 13th to the 15th centuries, using white clay obtained from Farnham Park. One of the potters was John Monger who died in 1604.

During the first half of the 19th century John Sheerin a butcher, Charles Stevens a glazier and painter, Daniel Smith a draper, John Spreadborough a tailor, William Page a thatcher and William Forrester a grocer were all at work in Ash. At Henley Park, servants, a coachman, a gamekeeper and a molecatcher were employed. Thomas Thompson was the village innkeeper, and there were some travellers in the area.

Meetings of the prominent persons of the village have been held in the church vestry for centuries. The civil duties of the vestry were taken over by the parish council in 1895. The rector was always the chairman of the vestry, and leading landowners such as Frederick Hammersley of Ash Grange, Henry Halsey of Henley Park, Dr. Chester of Poyle Park and John Lickfold of the Forge attended, as did Matthew Collins, the first schoolmaster at the National School. Churchwardens were elected to supervise the maintenance and repair of the church, and Waywardens or Surveyors of the Highway were chosen from amongst eligible landholders to take charge of the maintenance of the parish roads. The Surveyor had to arrange for all the men in the parish to do six days' work on the roads each year, although by the end of the 18th century most paid a fee instead. Farmers had to loan their carts and horses. In the 19th century the unemployed dug gravel and attempted to repair the worst places in the roads in return for support from the parish.

Much parish business concerned the operation of the Poor Law. Overseers and a Guardian were appointed each year. Elderly persons, widows, the wives and children of sick men, and the impoverished appealed to them for a few shillings a month to live on. When the price of bread was high, arrangements would be made to give them an extra loaf after church, and sometimes they were given the money for a pair of shoes. Only people born in Ash parish were supported. Those who moved into the parish were sent back home if they became paupers – thus in 1662 the Bignold family were sent back to Puttenham. This worked the other way too and in 1862 the parish faced a large bill for the return of John Blake and family from Chertsey to Ash.

The vestry also arranged entry to the workhouse, which was built well away from the rest of the village on the edge of the common. From 1790 both Ash and Puttenham parishes sent their paupers there and shared the costs. In the 1850s William Kight was master, and his salary was £40 per annum plus rations. His wife Elizabeth was matron.

A list of inmates is provided in the census of 1851: Robert Miles, a widower aged 72 and formerly a farmer (there was such a farmer living in Bricklyn who was an overseer in 1834); George Figg, aged 65, formerly a bricklayer; James Wheeler, 72, formerly a blacksmith; John Carter, farm labourer, his wife, daughter and baby; Maria Kercher, widow, her three children and baby; Elizabeth Hersey, her daughter and baby; Lucy Vollers, pauper, formerly house servant, and her baby; Emma Littleport aged six, place of birth not known; and Elizabeth Searle, aged ten. In the 1861 census there is just a sad list of initials, though it is clear that the Herseys are still living there. In 1870 the workhouse was closed, and from that time Ash paupers were sent to Farnham workhouse.

There were a number of parish charities, and these too were administered by the vestry. The food or fuel bought was distributed after church on specified days as a supplement to the relief given to the poor out of the rates. The oldest, of which the date and the giver had already been forgotten 200 years ago, was the rent of Parish Close, which was worth a lot when first given, as meadow was then valuable land. But the largest amount always came from Henry Smith's Charity which dates from 1653. Smith wanted paupers he supported to be distinguishable by wearing apparel of one colour marked with his initials, HS. Others included the five shillings a month worth of good wheaten bread paid for by the heirs of Thomas Stevens, who had made this a condition of their inheriting a meadow called Bannisters in Ash Green.

Village constables were first appointed in the Manor Courts, and later chosen by the vestry. All the men in the parish had to take a turn at this job, which included the prevention of crime, supervising punishments, collecting county rates and organising the local militia and their armour. Amongst criminals brought to the Assize Courts during the reigns of Elizabeth and James I was Stephen Ede, labourer of Ash, who was hanged for assaulting a traveller along the Hog's Back and stealing a purse containing £4 3s. 4d. Michael Russell, a tailor, was whipped for stealing several pieces of linen worth 10d., and Richard Jones received the same punishment for stealing a shirt worth 3d. and two neckerchiefs also worth 3d. Other thefts included a horse worth £5, a cow worth 16s., a brown bay gelding worth 5 marks (£1.66), and a nag worth 30s. Two young gentlemen from landowning families were accused of fighting in church and, worse still, a husbandman called George Mannory was murdered with a cudgel. In 1575 the curate was accused of the rape of 15-year-old Joan Collyns. He was found not guilty.

Less serious matters were settled at the Quarter Sessions. In the 1660s William Boylett, a yeoman, was in trouble for illegally building a barn on the highway between Ash Street and Farnham. Henry and Nicholas Stevens had obstructed a watercourse at Stotfold and Linsford Mead (Lynchford). Thomas Banckes had, on Sunday, allowed 'divers evil-disposed persons to gather at his house and to remain there, drinking and quarrelling, during the time of divine service'.

The coming of the railways through Ash and Ash Green in 1849 had a considerable impact on the village. Many railway employees moved into the area, such as Mr. MacKenzie, a railway contractor who came to live in Ash Street. The parish had sold a great deal of common land to the railway companies. The vestry discussed what to do with the money and considered using it to pay off the debt of £500 owed on the workhouse for 50 years. They also asked the railway companies to contribute to the rates and to pay for any parish gravel which they used.

In 1853 the decision was made to build a permanent army training camp at Aldershot. Common land in Ash parish was also purchased, and life was changed for ever in this area. The population of Ash jumped from 838 in 1851, to 1,481 in 1861, and thereafter continued to rise rapidly.

George Myers was a wealthy master builder who built the Royal Pavilion at Aldershot and the Staff College at Camberley. He opened up brickfields at Ash and his labourers and brickmakers came to live in the village. Since Aldershot station was not opened until 1870, Tongham, Ash and Ash Green railway stations were the nearest to the Camp. So Mr. Myers soon decided to run a single-track railway from the line near Tongham right into the barracks, and asked the vestry for permission to cross the parish roads in two places. This prompted them to ask him to pay rates, along with some of the other camp contractors. This they justified because of the enormous amount of damage being done to the unmade roads of Ash by the extra traffic going to the Camp, and by the soldiers marching.

Another notable effect on the village was the escalating number of public houses which sprang up all round the Camp. In 1851 there was only the *Greyhound*. By 1854 it had been joined by the *Dover Arms* and the *Railway Arms*, and in 1861 there were 16 pubs in Ash and Ash Common. Over the next two decades all those we know today had opened, together with a number of others which have since closed, for example the *Grenadier*, the *George and Dragon*, the *Duke of York* and the *Duke of Cambridge*. Perhaps it was just as well that Ash had a County Policeman, George Jewer, by 1853.

In 1858 the first child of a soldier was baptised in Ash church, the father being a sergeant in the Grenadier Guards camped on Ash Common. Before long army officers started to move into houses in the village. Captain Ellis lived in Paines Lane, Major General Carey at Shawfield House, and Lt. Crabbe and his family at Lower Ash Lodge. They were comfortably off, Lt. Crabbe employing a butler, head nurse, under nurse, nursemaid, housemaid and cook.

The common between Ash Wharf and Lynchford was rapidly becoming built up. It was known as Heath Vale in 1861, and a Congregational chapel had been built there opposite the *Admiral Napier*. The name Ash Vale had been coined by 1871. Many large houses were built for army officers at Ash Vale. Major Walker lived at Fairview, Sir Robert Haining at Chart House and Captain Brook at Northlands, and Hutton Road soon 'seemed like an army camp'.

Two businesses were started in Ash utilising the by-products of the large numbers of horses kept by the army. In 1861 there was the Manure Works at Ash Vale, and around 1865 William Bartram opened his Steam Bone Mills and Chemical Manure Company at Ash Bridge. The vestry soon had to write to him, complaining about the pollution he was causing in the river Blackwater, and he had to promise to stop 'his business draining into the river'.

Many tradesmen moved into the area. William Instone from Blackwater opened his smithy at Ash Common, and John Windibank of Alton opened a butcher's shop. John Emmings came from Newbury and set up as a greengrocer, and William Rattray from Scotland founded his nursery and sold flowers and seeds. A retired army veterinary surgeon called Theodore Charmbury established a photography business in Claremont Villa in Ash Vale. At the same time many new occupations were taken up by the locals. Robert Waters became a coal merchant, his business later becoming Scards, and Henry Murrell opened a pickle factory opposite Shawfields Recreation Ground. Yet, despite all these changes, many people were still working on farms well into the 20th century.

St Peter's church had already been altered in 1832 so that extra worshippers could be accommodated under the belfry, but because so many more people had moved into the area it became necessary in 1864 to add a large extension on the north side. Ash Vale's own church, St Mary's, was dedicated in 1885. Meanwhile Methodist chapels had opened in Wharf Road and Ash Street, and in 1934 Holy Angels church was built.

The National School opened in 1835 with 22 pupils. Ash Common School opened in 1860, and Ash Vale Council School in 1909, and by then there were about 624 scholars in the village. Although it had been enlarged over the years, by the 1900s the National School had again become overcrowded, with three classes being taught together in the main room. Damp and flooding had always been a problem at the school, and it was so bitterly cold in winter that the ink froze. Finally the building was condemned and in 1915 the master, William Daniel Read, transferred with all his pupils to a new building which became Walsh Memorial School. When the old school was demolished the timbers were salvaged and used in the construction of The Old Farmhouse in the Ash Hill Road.

From about 1855 to 1874 the landlord of the *Greyhound*, William Fountain, was also the village postmaster. The first post office was at Merryworth, where the letter box remained nailed to the front door for many years after it ceased to be used. A post office opened at Ash Vale *c.*1885, another at Pinewoods in 1896, and there was one at Ash Vale station by 1905. There were three posts a day during the week and one on Sundays. In 1907 William Brinkworth was given permission to close the Ash Vale branch at 12 noon on public holidays.

After the army came to Aldershot, the people of Ash were frequently treated to the sight of brightly uniformed soldiers marching through the village. In the 1870s and 1880s the army races at Aldershot were a good day out, and in 1874 everybody went to watch the military funeral of Captain Graham, who was buried in St Peter's churchyard. There were often Field Days and Sham Fights on the common, which were a marvellous spectacle. Best of all there were the Grand Reviews on the Foxhills or on Aldershot Common, which were presided over by Queen Victoria and other members of the British and foreign royal families. These were especially popular with the children, who so frequently missed school to watch that the masters often relented and gave them the time off anyway. The last Royal Review was in 1935, for King George's Silver Jubilee, and after that the children went to the Aldershot Tattoos.

Until World War Two a village fair took place on the green in front of the *Greyhound* on 21 June every year, with swings and roundabouts, stalls, and vehicles belonging to local businesses such as Scards the coal merchants. The village club held its anniversary celebrations in the *Greyhound* each May, there were regular circuses in Aldershot, and on May Day the children went garlanding. On Ascension Day there was the annual flower service at St Peter's church, when flowers were brought by all the children and sent to London hospitals. There were flower shows each July, bonfires were made on 5 November, and there were cricket matches to watch. In 1877 a ventriloquist entertained the children in the National School, and there were regular magic lantern shows there in the evenings, with views of London, the Egyptian Campaign and the Arctic Expedition, and Scenes from the life of Queen Victoria.

The school was also the venue, in 1881, for a lecture on the recently invented electric light, which included a demonstration. When the Moated Manor was sold in 1934 it had its own generator, and the sales particulars indicated that the mains cable was to be extended past the gates the following summer. Even in 1950 some of Lickfold's Cottages in Ash Street did not have electricity. Cleaning out wells had been a regular job earlier in the century. Mr. Woodman, the Ash builder, charged Mrs. Townsend of the Cannon 5s. 4d. to clean hers in 1907. The Frimley and Farnborough Water Company extended its mains as far as the canal bridge at Ash Wharf in 1898, and on via the *Dover Arms* to Ash Street and Oxenden Road four years later. By 1950 all the larger residential areas had piped water. Although the Parish Council discussed the collection of sewage as early as 1908 because odours from the cesspools in the village were creating a problem, there was opposition to improvements due to the excessive cost. It was not until the 1950s that new estates were built with mains drainage.

The new Ash Parish Council took up office in 1895. The first councillors included Frederick Britten who ran the West Surrey Printing Works at Prospect Villa, Charles Lickfold the blacksmith from the forge, and James McLaren who lived at Firacre and was manager of the Ash Vale Glue Factory. Over the years the Parish Council discussed many things we now take for granted. In 1903 a committee was formed to investigate the cost and necessity of street lighting. It was decided that 30 lamp posts were required, allowing for the light already given out by railway stations, inns and houses. Aldershot Gas and Water Company was prepared to supply and erect them for £150, and to maintain them for £3 per annum. They would be lit daily from 1 August to 31 May, and would not be extinguished before 11.30 p.m. Unfortunately the residents were reluctant to have the lights because it would mean an increase in their rates.

Following the Motor Car Act of 1903, the council decided that there were some 'dangerous zones' in Ash which required 'caution boards'. The *Dover Arms* corner, Box Cottage corner, the junction at the bottom of Church Walk and the junction between Government Road and the Vale Road were declared 'dangerous corners'. A speed limit of 10 miles per hour was imposed past Ash Vale School, between the *Greyhound* and St Peter's church, between the *King's Head* and the Grange, and from Lynchford Road to the *Anglers' Rest* corner. The councillors were very concerned about 'motor traffic with its attendant evils'.

In 1907 a special meeting was called to discuss the naming of roads in the parish. Some were to remain unchanged, such as Wharf Road, Station Road and Alexandra Road. However proposals to change Oxen Road to Downs Road, and Harpers Lane to Nightingale Road were unsuccessful, and some of the suggested names, like King Edward's Road (now Ash Hill Road), Deadbrook Road (now Shawfield Lane) and Recreation Road (now Balmoral Road) clearly did not catch on. In 1914 a committee was still endeavouring to obtain permission from owners to erect name plates in the selected places.

When war was declared in August 1914 everyone in the village was affected. The Parish Council formed a committee to deal with distress caused by the hostilities, school children began to darn and repair garments for the sick and wounded, and the Scouts became telegraph messengers and collected waste paper. The children at Ash Vale School cultivated a plot of land on the common and were allowed to go blackberrying during school hours, whilst a Food Control Committee was put in charge of food economy, and householders filled in forms for butter and margarine. Coal control pamphlets were distributed, and school hours were curtailed in winter as an economy measure.

There was much movement of British troops and equipment through the village, and residents watched as German prisoners of war were marched through to work, and as wounded soldiers from the Cambridge Hospital in Aldershot travelled along the canal for picnics in the fields near Ash Wharf. Armistice Day in 1918 was followed by peace celebrations, but most families in the village had lost at least one person in the Great War, and plans were soon underway for the War Memorial in the Ash Hill Road.

In the 1920s garden parties were held annually at Dene Lodge, and the village school children went to the British Empire exhibition at Wembley. In 1926 the first County Librarian addressed the annual parish meeting. Books would be sent free if the parish would provide accommodation and a librarian, so it was decided to open three libraries, at the Victoria Hall, Walsh Memorial School and Ash Vale School. In 1935 the first inoculations against diphtheria were given to children in Ash – many had died during past epidemics of this disease.

In 1938 the A.R.P. distributed gas masks. Then World War Two started and the children had to remember their gas masks at all times, and to come to school in shifts until sufficient shelter accommodation had been built. Evacuees came to the village and attended an extension school in the Victoria Hall. There were regular air raid warnings in 1940 and 1941, and again in 1944. During air raids the occupants of Mount Pleasant Cottages sheltered in the cellar of the *Lion Brewery* and members of the home guard did a clog dance on the cellar doors to sound the all clear. The local home guard had their headquarters at The Croft in Ash Green, and the Ash A.R.P. Wardens had a post at the *Bricklayers' Arms*. During the war a house in White Lane was hit by a bomb, and two houses in College Road were destroyed by one dropped at 2 o'clock in the morning. In case of invasion, tank traps were installed across the bridge at Ash Wharf and across Ash Street next to the Post Office, pill boxes were constructed, and holes were drilled in the railway bridges at Ash Green and Harpers Road so that they could be blown up. As a further precaution plans were made to billet 65 soldiers at Heathcote School. Fortunately none of this became necessary, the war finally ended, and V.E. Day was celebrated with fireworks and a huge bonfire at Ash Wharf.

After the war Ash grew steadily until in 1955 the parish was one of the most highly populated in the country, and the Boundary Commission decided that Normandy should become a separate parish. Now, in 1990, Ash has nearly 17,000 inhabitants, and the area has seen so much development that Ash Vale, Ash Common, Ash and Ash Green have merged almost completely. Ash has indeed seen many changes since it was a tiny rural community 150 years ago.

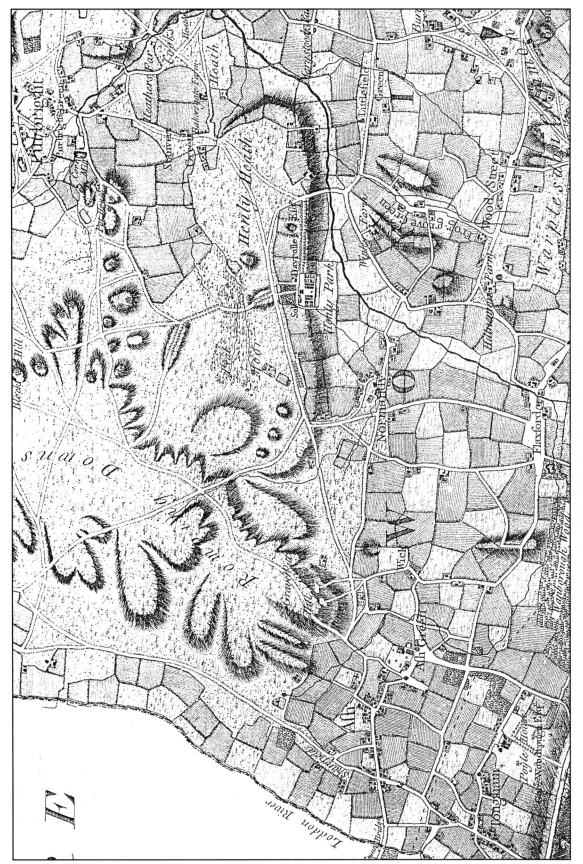

1. Ash in 1768, from Rocque's map of Surrey.

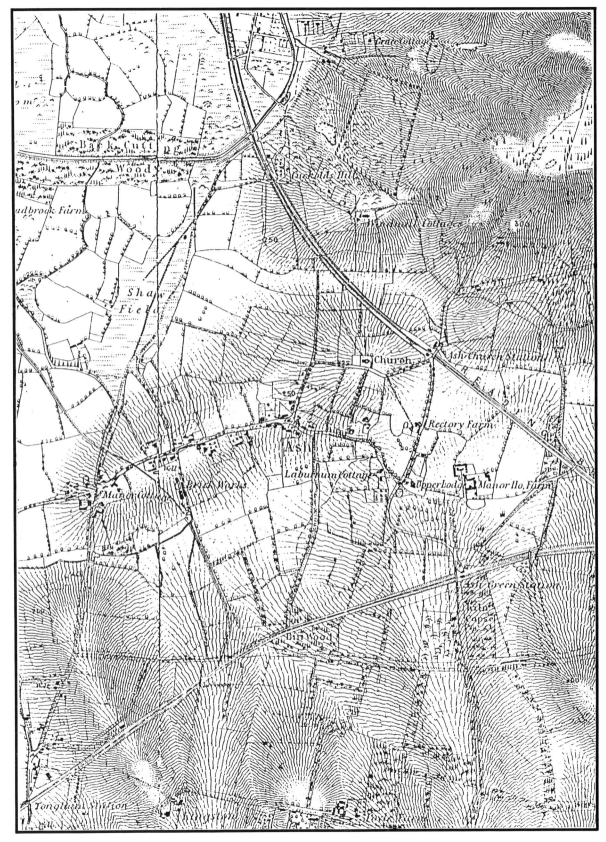

2. Ash in 1862.

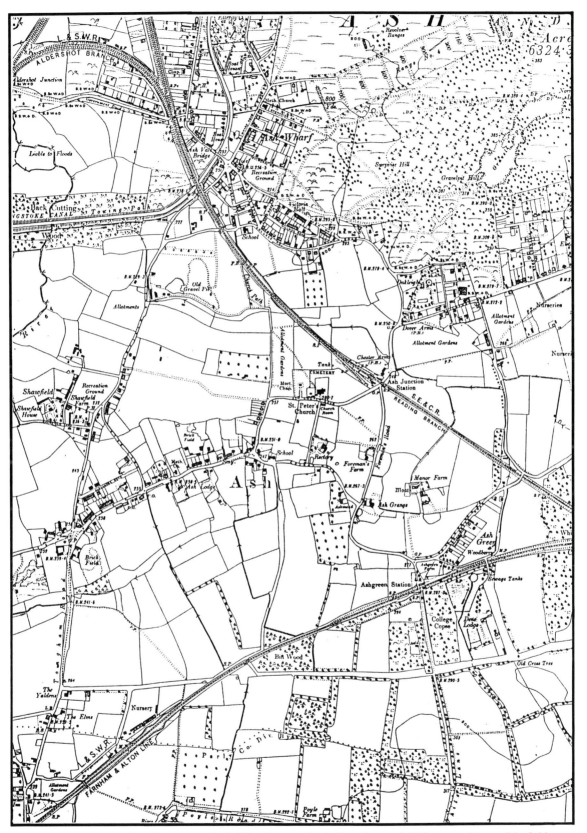

3. Ash in 1920, by which time a great deal of development had taken place at Ash Common. Many of the fields on this map are now the sites of housing estates.

4. The *Greyhound* public house, a 17th-century building where Friary Ales used to be sold. The name of the pub was probably derived from the coat of arms of the Gaynesford family, who owned Poyle Manor from 1440 to 1503, and the pub sign used to depict three greyhounds, just as there were on the coat of arms. The well known large oak tree stood in front of the *Greyhound* in the middle of the crossroads before the present roundabout was constructed. Fern Cottages can be seen behind the pub in Shawfield Road.

5. Manor Road in 1932, with Merryworth on the left. This house was built *c.*1510, and has a priest's hole, where a certain Father Jenkins is said to have hidden before he was caught and put to death. In the 19th century this was William Faggotter's farm, whilst some more recent owners ran a kennels, bred cocker spaniels, and created a dog cemetery.

6. Children on the village green at Manor Road in September 1921.

7. This coach builder's works was on the corner now occupied by the Greyhound Close flats. The proprietor, Mr. Robert Harris, is the man with the dogs, his blacksmith is on the left, and the carts are examples of those made at the works. Sitting in the baker's van is Mr. Hawes of the post office, whose son Albert is standing with the barrow. The roof in the background is part of Pratt's Farm, which lay further along the Aldershot Road, and the building on the right is Japonica Cottage.

R. HARRIS,

Coach & Motor Builder,

Carpenter, Wheelwright & Undertaker,

Shoeing and General Smith.

CYCLE AGENT.

—

CARTS, VANS, WAGGONS, MADE TO ORDER.

—

Japonica Works, ASH.

Repairs of all descriptions. Prompt attention to all Customers

8. This advertisement for Japonica Works appeared in St Peter's parish magazine in December 1909.

9. In later years the business became known as the Always Welding, manufacturing small numbers of vehicles such as dustcarts and petrol tankers. The picturesque old farmhouse of Pratt's Farm was by then being used as offices.

ALWAYS WELDING
LIMITED

★   ★   ★

STEEL FABRICATORS

Manufacturers and Suppliers of:

ROAD TANKERS FOR TRANSPORTATION
OF PETROLEUM, FUEL OILS, ETC.

COMMERCIAL VEHICLE BODYWORK
AND OIL STORAGE TANKS.

PRODUCTS MANUFACTURED TO
CUSTOMERS INDIVIDUAL REQUIREMENTS

★   ★   ★

Contractors to Admiralty and Crown Agents

★   ★   ★

ASHE WORKS, ASH
Nr. ALDERSHOT

Telephone: ALDERSHOT 20241/2/3
Telegrams: "ALWELD", ALDERSHOT

10. Advertisement for Always Welding.

11.   Reynold's Cottages in Shawfield Road, *c*.1935. These cottages stood opposite what is now the Shawfield Day Centre, and their gardens stretched back to Alexandra Road. They were the homes of agricultural labourers.

12.   Bartrams County Bridge Steam Bone Mills and Chemical Manure Works was opened *c*.1865. The house in the picture was built in 1869, and the bricks were made on the site from clay dug there. Because of Bartrams, the sewage works and the gas works, the area used to be known as smelly corner.

13. The *Bricklayers' Arms* public house is an 18th-century building, which was originally three cottages. Bricks made in the vicinity were used for building the barracks at Aldershot Camp, and were transported on a railway track from Tongham which crossed Ash Street next to the pub. The picture dates from *c*.1920.

14. Ash Street in the 1950s, with the *Bricklayers' Arms* and Crooke's cottages on the right. Messrs. Crooke, Brewers of Guildford, opened the pub in 1855. Their brewery, which was opposite St Nicholas's church in Guildford, was sold to Hodgson's of Kingston in 1925, and eventually became part of Courage.

15. Bricklyn in Ash Street is now called Azor Place. The oldest part was built *c*.1568, and faced with bricks when the east wing was added in 1717. This house has a sun dial and a Royal Fire Exchange insurance plate, and used to be a farm with two ponds.

16. Herbert Langley Ward, a local builder, bought Bricklyn in 1925. He fitted a fireplace which had come from Poyle Park and displayed the crest of the Woodroffe family. He made some other alterations, including the conversion of the bacon curing loft into a cupboard and laying out the gardens. Mr. Ward is one of the Special Constables in plate 42, and this is a memo he sent in 1923.

H. L. WARD, F.B.I.C.C.
F. B. WARD.

Memo. from **WARD** & **WARD**

Builders, : Decorators : and : Sanitary : Engineers.

REPAIRS AT MODERATE PRICES.　　ESTIMATES FREE.

17. Mr. Ward used the barn behind Bricklyn for his building business. It was later converted into two houses called Barn Hatch.

18. In 1961 Mr. Ward sold half an acre of his land to Surrey County Council, and Ash Library was built there. The building itself is on top of what used to be a pond which had been used as a dump, whilst the car park occupies a field where chickens and bantams used to be kept. The area has recently been greatly altered by the addition of accommodation for Social Services on the site.

19 This building is now the Post Office and Stores in Ash Street, and dates from the 16th and 17th centuries. Joseph Hawes ran a grocery store here from the 1880s. His son Albert Hawes (on the cart in plate 7), ran the business after him, followed by his grandsons James and Bob.

119   *ASH STREET,*
ASH,.............................189...

With Compliments

Received from   *Mr Gateum*

on Account of **J. HAWES,** the *sum* of   *10/—*

Por..... *note of P....*.........................*Pence.*

Signature........*J Hawes*.....

and best thanks.

£   *10*   s.   *0*   d.

20. A receipt issued by Joseph Hawes, who can be seen in plate 58.

21. This advertisement appeared in 1909 when Mr. Horne had become a partner in the business. By this time the shop had become the village post office. The Daren bread which was so popular was a type of brown bread made with Daren flour.

HAWES & HORNE,

High-class Family Bakers & Grocers

ASH STREET, ASH

And at NORMANDY.

Awarded Second Prize, Bakers' Exhibition, 1896, for Daren Bread. Awarded Bronze Medal, Bakers' Exhibition, 1900, for Malted Brown Bread ; and Gold Medal, Master Bakers' Society, 1901, for Tin Bread.

"DAREN" BREAD

Has been Awarded 83 Honours

22. Tilthams Garage and Cleveland Cars are now on the site of this large pond next to the Post Office, where James Hawes used to wash his cart. This picture dates from *c*.1905. Locals can remember wet fish and vegetables on sale in the shack on the side of the building.

23. By 1908 an extension had been added at the front of the shop. It is just visible in this picture.

24. The village Post Office and Stores in 1932, after the pond had been filled and the road made up. You can see the hedge of the land where the library is now, where James Hawes used to keep his horse. By this time the shop had its first telephone number, Aldershot 150.

25. Tudor House in Ash Street is a 16th-century building with an interesting Sun Alliance fire insurance plaque. Fire insurance was taken out in 1783 by the tenant George May, yeoman of Ash. Building cover was provided to the value of £150, contents cover to £50, and his barn was insured for £100. The house still contains part of a bacon smoking chamber.

26. This old timber-framed house was dilapidated and unoccupied when this photograph was taken in October 1921. It was in Ash Street and is thought to have been approximately where Walter's Handyman Stores are now.

27. Lavender Cottage in Ash Street is an early 17th-century building. The west wall is patterned with flints, but is obscured by the house next door.

28. Ash Street *c*.1905. Lickfold's Cottages are on the right, with the smithy projecting out to the edge of the road. John Lickfold was the blacksmith in the mid-19th century, and Charles Lickfold, who has the distinction of being one of the first Ash Parish Councillors, was blacksmith at the turn of the century. In the field on the left of the picture, behind the barn, is Lavender Cottage.

29. This advertisement for the Forge dates from 1925 and shows that Stephenson and Bembridge were undertakers as well as blacksmiths. Wilfred Stephenson can be seen in plate 42.

STEPHENSON
AND
BEMBRIDGE

PHONE : ASH VALE 76

FUNERALS COMPLETELY FURNISHED
: at Moderate Charges. :

THE FORGE———ASH STREET
ASH, SURREY

30. This picture was taken at the end of the harvest in about 1905. The man with the boater and cigar standing in front of the horse is Reginald Bateman who farmed at Ash Lodge Farm from *c*.1890-1905. Reginald was the youngest son of William Bateman, who can be seen in picture 74.

31. Lickfold's Cottages and the Forge, c.1908. These 'quaint country cottages' were brick-built with roofs partly of slate and partly tiled, and there were exposed timbers in some of the walls and ceilings. In the distance is the Ash Street Methodist chapel, the site of which is now occupied by Clare Court.

32. Mrs. Boxall standing outside No.3 Lickfold's Cottages.

D. DEWHURST

Agricultural & Automobile Engineer

AUTOMOBILE SPRING SPECIALIST

Shoeing and General Smith — General Car Repairs
Electrical and Acetylene Welding

AGENT FOR EAGLE INSURANCE CO., LTD.

The Forge, Ash Street, ASH

Telephone :
Ash Vale 2314

33.   An advertisement for D. Dewhurst in 1953. Mr. Dewhurst had taken over the business in 1947. In 1960 both the forge and the cottages were condemned by the council and Dewhurst was forced to demolish them. The house called Brimmond was then built for his family to live in, and the Forge Works moved to its present position behind.

34.   The Forge Garage in the 1950s, with some fascinating old advertisements displayed. The signs on the front offer an Aladdin Pink Paraffin delivery service, whilst the sign in the top left of the window encourages customers to have their brakes tested regularly. The spire of St Peter's church can be seen in the background, and the *Cannon* is selling Courage & Barclays brew.

35.   A glimpse of the interior of the old smithy in the 1950s. It was still operational until the late 1950s.

36.   Another picture of the interior of the forge.

37.   This picture of part of Ivy Cottage was taken *c.*1940, when the Dewhursts lived there. Ivy Cottage lay behind the old forge, and was approached by the lane which leads to the present Forge Works.

38. The Poplars, a house with a distinctive row of trees in front of it, was the residence of Mr. John Stedman, census enumerator for Ash in 1881 and Sanitary Officer in 1884 during a very serious diphtheria epidemic. He was also Clerk to Ash Parish Council from 1895 to 1903, Overseer and Assessor of the Queens's Taxes, Surveyor to Farnham Rural District Council, and a churchwarden at St Peter's.

39. Rear view of the Poplars, which many will recognise as the beer garden of the *King's Head* in Ash Street. The Poplars became a pub when Mr. Pat Maloney (one of the wardens in plate 113) lived there.

40. John Stedman's son Wilfred became a brickmaker and lived at Breelands in Aldershot Road. This is a receipt for 200 rough stock bricks which he sold in 1909.

Telephone : 136 x.

ASH ROAD BRICK WORKS.

No 598 .... June 4 190 9

Messrs Gatcum & Sons ....

Received from WILFRED T. STEDMAN,

....Fine Gravel
....Coarse ditto
....Concrete ditto
....Shingle
....Ballast
....Clay
....Sand
....Top Soil
....Breeze
....Foreman.

41. The original *King's Head*, *c.*1920, a small building between the Poplars and April Cottage. The pub had been called the *Railway Arms* when it first opened *c.*1854, but the name soon changed. Walter Woodman was landlord, and his eldest son William became a very well known builder in the area. The pub was tied to Crooke and Co. of Guildford, and appears to have offered special facilities for cyclists.

42.   Ash Section, 'C' Division, Surrey Special Constabulary. July 1935. *Front row*: W. G. Penn, J. H. Nixon, D/Sec. Leader F. H. Young (landlord of the *Cannon*), Div. Leader W. E. Loe, Sgt. W. Budd of the Surrey Constabulary (whose leather truncheon is now owned by his next door neighbour at Park Villas), Section Leader F. Gilbert, A. Hillary (furniture dealer of Hillary's Stores), P. E. Flynn and S. Froud. *Back row*: F. G. W. Young (son of the other Young), C. D. Manfield (of Box Farm), Herbert L. Ward (builder of Bricklyn), Frank B. Ward (Herbert's brother), F. W. Berry (of Grange Road), J. Smith (who lived in April Cottage and worked at Bides Nursery), F. L. Jeffery, R. Harrison (who lived at Corté, Ash Street), A. O. Jones and W. E. Stephenson (blacksmith at the Forge).

43. Ash Street *c*.1905, with the *Cannon* on the right. The pub sign can be seen on the opposite side of the road, where it stood in the middle of a large pond called 'Broadlake'. The building became a beerhouse in 1859, when Daniel Manfield was landlord, and was tied to Farnham United Breweries. On the right of the *Cannon* was a shop selling sweets and groceries, where a pennyworth of treacle in a cone made by twisting a piece of paper at one end could be bought. The shop was demolished in about 1920.

44. John Hassell painted this watercolour in 1824. He and his son painted over 2,000 Surrey views. The road is now Ash Church Road, between Church View and Ash Street, and none of the buildings has survived. In the position now occupied by Sharrocks stood Box Cottage, where Daniel Manfield lived after he left the *Cannon*.

The Executors of the late   Established 1859

GEORGE MANFIELD,

Coal and Coke Merchants,

Railway Station, Ash, S.E.R.

All Goods Delivered at Lowest Possible Prices.

Orders to be addressed to Box Cottage, Ash

45. Daniel Manfield's son George, a farmer and coal merchant, was Parish Clerk from 1871-1908. This advertisement dates from 1909.

46. Cream from the Box Farm dairy was bought by Grandma Evans to make the ice cream sold in her café in the Limes, a house opposite the farm where Lime Crescent is now. This advertisement dates from 1925. Daniel Manfield's grandson Cuthbert, one of the Special Constables in plate 42, was Chairman of the Ash Parish Council from 1925-8 and from 1939-45.

The Exors. of the late

G. MANFIELD

BOX FARM 'DAIRY
—ASH—

Pure New Milk

direct from our own Farm

CREAM
EGGS
BUTTER

47. Ash National School was opened in 1835 and stood opposite South Lane in what is now Grange Road. A pair of cottages had been converted into one room with a brick floor, and there was a gravel yard outside. An infants' room was added at the east end in 1872, and the classroom at the west end was built in 1884. This picture was painted by John J. Miles, one of the masters at the school, who can be seen in plate 58.

48. The school stamp as it appears in the front of the old Log Books, in which the masters recorded day-to-day events.

49. Rectory Lodge in Grange Road (now Glebe Cottage), was occupied by successive school masters and their families. The first was Matthew Collins, who was also one of the guardians in charge of the parish poor, and whose wife was school mistress. He was followed by Thomas Phillips, and later by John Miles who was master for 18½ years before moving to Ash Common School in 1897. Sadly, this house has now been demolished.

50. Walsh Memorial School, which opened in January 1915. Mr. Hawes, who lived opposite in Crooksbury View, remembers the event, because the Bishop put on his robes in the Hawes' house, and the little boy couldn't resist trying on his mitre.

51. Yeomans Bridge Secondary Modern School, which has now become Ash Manor School. The temporary buildings on the left, which were first occupied in 1950, have now been demolished. The school was originally named after the bridge in the foreground of the picture, which crossed the stream at a ford which was 20ft. wide and 6ins. deep. The bridge was mentioned in Court Rolls as early as 1511, when it was referred to as 'Youngmansbryge'.

52. This is a typical class photograph, taken at Walsh Memorial School. Mrs. Johnson was the teacher, and George Moore is the little boy on the left in the back row. He lived at Smith's Cottages in Ash Street, near to the Post Office.

53. St Peter's church, *c.*1820. The wooden south porch was later bricked in. The roof was of Horsham slate, and the large low tower with stone battlements had a short, slender spire covered with lead. The church was enlarged in 1864, at a cost of £3,000.

54. This water colour, painted by Edward Hassell in the early 19th century, shows the windows which were in the north wall before the church was enlarged. The pulpit was made of oak and carved in the style of James I's reign, and the sounding board is visible above. Hassell also painted four small pictures showing the carving of the rood screen in more detail, the pattern of which has been copied in the new part of the church.

55.   This picture of the church dates from *c*.1900, and shows some of the drive leading to the Rectory. Perhaps the boys in the picture were on their way to the National School.

56.   St Peter's church *c*.1905. The striking clock on the tower had not yet been given by Dr. Chester, and there was a lamp over the gateway. In the foreground is Church Walk, a neat gravel drive leading to the Rectory, which had gates at both ends. As can be seen, there were gaps large enough to walk through, because there had always been a public right of way.

57. The wedding of Charles Bateman and Emily Newnham, which took place at St Peter's church in February 1897. The bride is sitting centre front, with the bridegroom just behind her. Seated on either side of the bride are the groom's parents, Matthew Bateman, a builder from Ash Vale, and his wife Alice.

58. This photograph was taken outside St Peter's church, *c*.1909. From left to right, *seated*: Reverend Walsh, Mr. J. J. Miles (Headmaster at Heathcote School), Mr. Thomas Osgood (Parish Councillor and farmer), Mr. Robert Brooke (baker at Ash Common), and the Reverend Lacey. *Standing*: Mr. Wild, Mr. R. Hunt (builder), Mr. Joseph Hawes (proprietor of Hawes & Horne), and Mr. Bishop. Messrs. Brooke, Hawes, Osgood, Miles and Wild were all sidesmen at the church.

59. The Reverend George Lamont
Cole, M.A., Rector of St Peter's from
1925 to 1930.

60. The bells of St Peter's were recast
and hung on a new steel frame in 1950.
One of the engineers is pictured, with
Mrs. Pepler, the secretary of the group
of ringers who raised the £1,000
needed for the work, and the Reverend
Harold Maurant Insley, Rector from
1945 to 1964.

61. The tomb of Arnald Brocas, Rector until 1368. He was afterwards Rector of St Nicholas' church at Guildford, where his tomb can be seen in the Loseley Chapel. His effigy shows him in a long red robe with a dog at his feet, and the inscription on a brass strip records his death in 1395.

62. Hartshorn (Ash Church Road) in 1904, during the restorations which are recorded on a plaque on the east gable end. Dr. Chester of Poyle was then the owner of the cottage, and a shield bearing the Arms of Chester quartering Woodroffe was also erected. The barn in the picture was very old, and in about 1926 it suddenly fell down and the rubble was used to fill in the well in the garden of Hartshorn, which at 100ft. deep was said to be the deepest in Ash.

63. Another view of Hartshorn in 1904. Possibly it was Dr. Chester's car which was parked in front.

64. The Old Rectory. The front was built in 1720, and behind is a large Elizabethan building.

From an engraving by J. Collyer.

65. The poet Edward Young, who wrote one of his best known poems whilst staying with his brother-in-law, the Reverend John Harris, at Ash Rectory. It was called *Night Thoughts on Life, Death and Immortality*, was 10,000 lines long and was produced in nine books between 1742-5. There had been three deaths in the family, and Young sat up all night writing because he could not sleep.

66. Reverend Albert Octavius Walsh with his family, standing at the door of the Old Rectory in 1886. Reverend Walsh was Rector of Ash from 1884 until 1916.

67. Ash Manor, at Ash Green, *c.*1908. The eastern part of the building, in the foreground, is the oldest and contains massive oak beams. The west wing and the large central chimney were built by Nicholas Stevens in 1657, who added a plaque bearing his initials and the date. This wing still contains a remarkable Jacobean staircase.

68. Ash Manor in 1932, shortly before it was restored and modernised. The Georgian tiled front, windows and porch were then removed, revealing the old timbers and herringbone brickwork. After the renovations, Maurice Kelly bought the house and it was he who called in an American medium to release the ghost of Lord Henley, which it was claimed had been imprisoned in the house for 400 years.

69. The lounge at Ash Manor, *c*.1934. This is the room where courts would once have been held.

70. The oast house at Ash Manor. Behind it is a large barn which dates from *c*.1500.

71. Sale of Ash Manor House, June 1934

72. Ash Green Farm in about 1870. The farmer with the shot-gun is William Bateman. His second wife Elizabeth is sitting by the wall, and their two young sons, George Gurney and Ernest, can also be seen. The house is now called The Old Farmhouse and is in Drovers Road.

73. William Bateman outside the front door of Ash Manor, c.1895, looking very much the gentleman farmer. Mr. Bateman farmed at Ash Manor from c.1874 until he retired at the turn of the century and handed over to his son, George Gurney. He spent the last years of his life at Ash Green Farm again.

74. This wonderful portrait of William Bateman was taken in 1908, when he was 90 years old. He had begun his career as a labourer and gamekeeper before becoming one of the most important farmers in the village.

75. William Bateman and his daughter Hannah at Ash Green Farm on 30 July 1907.

76. Laburnum Cottage in 1905, complete with laburnum tree. John Roger and Sarah Hodgskin, one of William Bateman's daughters, are standing in front of the house. The Hodgskins ran a poultry farm, and their free-range chickens roamed all over Parish Close behind the house. Alfred Parsons moved into Laburnum Cottage in about 1911 and renamed it Ashmead. Ashmead is in Grange Road.

77. Ash Green station, disused and overgrown, but with one of the tracks still in place. The line was opened in 1849, and closed to passengers in 1937. It is said that Queen Victoria once alighted at Ash Green station on her way to review her troops at Aldershot, and that she was accompanied by Prime Minister Gladstone who was visiting Wanborough church.

78. Ash Grange (formerly Ash Lodge) was built for William Spode of the Staffordshire pottery family, who retired to Ash *c.*1811. Spode changed his name to Hammersley, and his memorial and funeral hatchment can be seen in St Peter's church. His son, who was born in Ash, emigrated to Australia and became a famous sportsman and helped frame the Australian Football Rules Code. Major-General Frederick Hammersley, who founded the Army School of Physical Training at Aldershot, also lived in the house.

79. The stables at Ash Grange. Ash Grange is in Foreman Road, at the junction with Grange Road.

80. This photograph is taken from an early home movie made during one of the garden parties which were held at Dene Lodge in Ash Green in the 1920s. Almost the whole of Ash attended, and the children of Heathcote School put on dancing displays. Andus Eric K. Cull, a Swedish millionaire stockbroker, lived at Dene Lodge with his wife, who was from the American Rothschild family, and their seven children.

81. The Thatched Cottage at Ash Green. Mr. Cull had the house built in 1929 as a home for the gardener at Dene Lodge. The thatch was destroyed by fire in 1988, and the house now has a tiled roof.

82. Part of Butt Inhams at Ash Green, four cottages built for the other employees at Dene Lodge. The butler lived at No.1, the chauffeur at No.2, and the groom at No.3. These houses were built by Mr. Ward of Bricklyn.

83. The old cross tree in Ash Green Lane East in 1985, before it finally fell down. This huge oak got its name because it grew at the meeting point of two old green ways. It also marked the boundary between Ash and Wyke.

84. The level crossing at Ash station, before the road was made up. The *Chester Arms* can be seen next to the station. The public house was named after the Chester family, and their coat of arms is set into the wall at the front of the building. The brewery was Thomas Kenward's of Hartley Row.

85. This picture of steam trains in Ash station was taken *c.*1934. The sign reads 'Ash change for Aldershot Town'. The trains belonged to the London and South Western Railway Company. As can be seen, Ash was once a much busier station than it is today, with sidings which have now been removed.

86. In this view down the line at Ash station the old engine shed can be seen on the right. It has now been converted into offices, and forms part of a small industrial estate.

87. The water tower at Ash station. Water was pumped from the well on the left of the picture and stored in a cast-iron tank. The water tower was rediscovered in 1986, having been hidden by trees and ivy for many years. Unfortunately, it has now been removed.

88. Foreman Manor in Foreman Road. This house was built in about 1854 for Henry Chester, who had just inherited Poyle Manor in Tongham together with considerable land in Ash. The house has his coat of arms carved in stone over the front door, and the initials of his two sons on plaques on the front.

89. This picture of the *Duke of York* in Harpers Road was taken before Pine Cottages were built opposite in 1903. Previously known as Shortlands Cottage, the building became a public house in the 1850s and sold beer from the Friary Brewery in Guildford. The landlord lost his licence in about 1907 because it was a rowdy house.

90. The Esdaile family from London, who bred goats, took up residence in 1911, and renamed the old pub York House. In this picture, taken about 1915, Grandfather Esdaile is sitting in the garden with the dog. York Cottage, the part of the building nearest the road, was later the home of Violet Johnson of the Harmony Sisters (plate 94).

91. Beer being delivered by horse and cart to the *Lion Brewery* in the Guildford Road in 1906. The sign on the pub advertises 'Entire', a variety of beer brewed since the early 18th century. In 1892 the *Lion Brewery* was a free house run by Rosina Fountain, but it was later tied to Hodgson's Kingston Brewery Company. Mount Pleasant Cottages are on the left, and the *Nightingale* pub is just visible up the road.

92. Mrs. Beat Jenkins, the wife of the landlord Jim Jenkins, standing outside the *Lion Brewery* with a group of regulars. Mrs. Jenkins' parents, the Cathralls, had come to the pub in about 1911 from the *Lamb* in the West End of Aldershot. Mr. Jenkins took over the licence in 1923.

93. Mr. Jenkins arranged outings by charabanc to the seaside, and took barrels of beer along. This picture was taken in Southsea in 1921, and shows Mr. Jenkins sitting behind the man with the bowler hat. Sadly he died in 1940, but his wife continued to run the pub, with the help of her daughter Beatie Hodgkinson, until she retired in 1954.

94. Beatie Hodgkinson is best known for her accordion playing, and she still performs at the local Red Cross Centre, the Day Centre and the Blind Club. In the 1930s she played with Violet Johnson of York Cottage and they were known as the Harmony Sisters. The photograph was taken at the Wigan Hippodrome in 1938. During the war they travelled widely and were very popular at troop concerts. Violet finally joined Vera Lynn's group of entertainers.

95.   Pinewoods Post Office, which was opened in 1896 in the building which is now the Guildford Road Newsagents. James Pryor was grocer and postmaster and, when he retired after the Great War, the Post Office was transferred to the present building. At this point Mr. Pryor's daughter, who was the organist at Wyke church, turned the shop into a drapery and haberdashery known as Selfridges Stores. This picture dates from 1906.

96.   Stone Cottages in the Guildford Road, which date from the 18th century.

97. The *Dover Arms*, at the junction of Guildford Road and Ash Hill Road, was opened *c.*1854 and sold beer brewed by Thomas Kenward and Company of Hartley Row.

98. The Dover Garage was built in 1923 by Mr. Ernest Woodman. The site was a meadow where cricket matches used to be played, and cricket was also played in the nearby fields where Fairview Road is now. Ernest Woodman was one of the players who was once sheltering under a tree there when it was struck by lightning.

99. An advertisement for the garage which appeared in 1925, soon after it opened.

100.   The Ash United 2nd XI Cricket Team in 1928. From left to right, *standing*: Arthur Glover (umpire), Jack Clifford, George Clarke, Ernie Saunders, Bill Broadhead, Mr. Joynes, Les Joynes, unidentified, Arthur Taylor. *Seated*: Bill Harris, Harry Sherman, Jim Burt, J. Barton, Jack Roffey. *Sitting on the ground*: Frank Burt.

101.   The workhouse at Ash in the early 19th century, painted by Edward Hassell. There were three buildings, of which this was the largest. In 1870 the workhouse was closed and sold.

102.   This house, although much altered, was part of the same workhouse building. It was known as Vine House, and the gable end bore a plaque with the date 1810. In the garden was a low stone out-building which had once belonged to the workhouse. Both buildings were demolished *c.*1967 to make way for new houses.

103.   Hunters Lodge in Foxhills Road, another of the workhouse buildings. This is now the only one remaining.

104. If you were looking at this view today, you would be standing in the middle of Ash Hill Road, with Fairview Road on your left. This was Hillside Farm run by James Hogsflesh and after him by his son Luke, Chairman of the Parish Council from 1921-2. William Wren, who was Clerk to the Parish Council from 1907 to 1941, lived in Farmside, the big house facing down the hill. The photograph was taken in 1906.

105. Joe Johnson the dairyman had his cowstalls in the fields where Fairview Road is today. His advertisement dates from 1909.

The Dairy, Ash Common.

J. JOHNSON,

𝔓𝔲𝔯𝔳𝔢𝔶𝔬𝔯 𝔬𝔣 𝔥𝔦𝔤𝔥=𝔠𝔩𝔞𝔰𝔰 𝔇𝔞𝔦𝔯𝔶 𝔓𝔯𝔬𝔡𝔲𝔠𝔢

Families waited on twice daily.

All Milk produced at Hillside Farm.

106. The War Memorial in the Ash Hill Road when it was unveiled on Easter Sunday in 1921. The Reverend Lambrick, rector at St Peter's church from 1916-25, is standing on the right. The stone cross cost £350, but the piece of land was the gift of Isaac Field, who kept a sweet shop at Heatherly Cottages, where the Empire Video Shop is now. His son Ernest was to have had a market garden there, but sadly he was killed in action during the war.

107. The War Memorial after the wreaths had been laid, looking in the other direction. The Ash Scouts are in the front row. In the background the trees on the common are still quite small.

108. Harold Somerville, who was a scout in the Ash Group c.1912. The scouts used to camp on the common and in the field where Manfield School is now. In 1914 the scoutmaster, Mr. Read, went to join up, and the scouts became telegraph messengers and collected waste paper.

109. No. 1 Platoon, 'B' Coy. 2nd Surrey Bn. Home Guard. *Back row*: A. Knight (of Ash Green), H. Stocker, M. Goddard, J. Penhaligon, G. Harris, J. Wheeler, A. Meech, P. Lovett, W. Johnson, A. Bundy. *Middle row*: R. Murrell, C. J. Whelan, J. Chalcroft, J. Callingham (of St Georges Stores), P. Lyddall, C. Barltrop, A. Ware, R. Lambert, W. Goddard, P. Maloney (of Poplar Villas in Grange Road), A. Wakefield, C. Jacobs, R. Dyson. *Front row*: Cpl. D. G. Bailey, Cpl. E. France (of Park Villas in Ash Street), Sgt. A. Campbell, Sgt. R. Jacobs, Sgt. C. Stapleton, 2/Lt. A. J. Drewitt (of Ash Church Road), 2/Lt. C. J. Smith (of Ash Green), Sgt. T. Armes (of Star Lane), Sgt. T. Prior (postman), Cpl. W. Ratcliffe, Cpl. J. H. Bullen (of Alexandra Road), Cpl. A. Noakes (of Ash Vale).

110.   This party to celebrate the Silver Jubilee of King George V and Queen Mary was held in the Victoria Hall in 1935.
Mrs. Kercher has been identified sitting third from the right in the front row, with Mr. Kercher behind her. Also in the
front row, sixth from the right, is Mrs. Flora Mercer. Behind her and peeping round the man with the moustache is Mrs.
Philpotts. Mr. and Mrs. Maskell are at the far end of the table on the left, and Mrs. Thompson is the third lady back in
the row against the right hand wall.

111. The Victoria Hall in the Ash Hill Road in the very bad winter of 1947. The hall was built to commemorate the Diamond Jubilee of Queen Victoria in 1897. The architect was H. J. Stedman and the builder was W. J. Woodman, his tender being £475. Dr. Chester, who owned Poyle Park, bought the land and laid the foundation stone. Later he provided the clock in memory of his mother, paid for the billiards room, the chairs, the fire buckets and for the connection of a water supply.

112. Mrs Hawes' A.R.P. Identification Card.

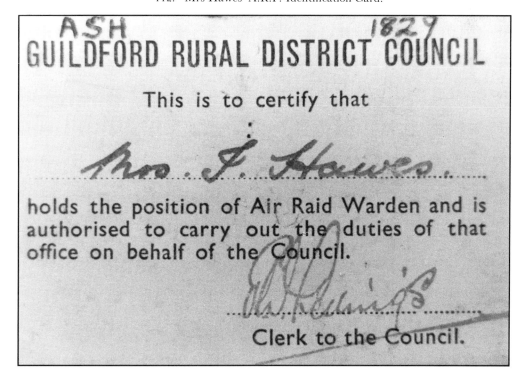

113. The Ash Wardens outside the Victoria Hall in 1943. From left to right. *In the front row*: The messenger boys Bob Noakes; Bert Hawes (now in Canada); Harold Brewer (baker's boy) and two from Ash Vale. *Second row*: Jim Moore (standing); unidentified; Mrs. Rose (of Crookes Cottages); George Neil (of Neil's Stores opposite Walsh School); Sid Hoare (of Pinewood Road); Mr. Franklin (of College Road); unidentified; Joe Hawes, the Chief Warden; unidentified; Arthur Hillary (of the Stores); Mr. Caney and his wife (a vet, of White Lane Ash Green); Iris Hawes (of Ash Street Post Office and Stores). *Third row*: First five and behind unidentified; Jack Ralph, behind; Harry Drain with Bob Hawes behind; Ern Harris (coal merchant of Shawfield Road) with Mr. Stanley (of Temperance Villas, Ash Street) behind; Harry Brooks (chimney sweep) with George Smith (of Rosewood Cottages) behind; Tom Bunker (baker and postmaster); unidentified; Jack Harwood (of Ash Green). *Back row*: Mr. Prescott (of White Lane and vegetable shop in Aldershot Arcade); Pat Maloney; Mr. Bond (of Star Lane); Norman Coleman (of Carfax); unidentified; John Ward (of South Lane); Tony Coe (of Star Lane, and an Aldershot Councillor); unidentified; Fred Allden (of Alexandra Road); Alf Kercher (whose son later ran the stores in Longacre).

114. Ash Common School in College Road was the second school to be built in Ash. It was opened in 1860, at a time when the population in the area was rapidly increasing. An extra room was added in 1884, paid for by the Reverend Heathcote, who had been rector for 46 years. In 1897 the school was again enlarged, and it was renamed Heathcote School. This picture was taken in 1905.

115.   Standard I in their classroom at Heathcote School in 1928.

116. The Ash Daffodil Bazaar was held in order to raise money for the 'School Enlargement Fund'. The local newspaper reported that 'the greatest activity prevailed upon the arrival of their Royal Highnesses the Duke and Duchess of Connaught, and both their Royal Highnesses appeared highly pleased with the loyal reception accorded to them'. Arthur, Duke of Connaught, was General Officer Commanding at Aldershot Camp at that time.

117. Windmill railway crossing before Shawfield footbridge replaced it. Many people remember Mrs. Kelly, the crossing keeper, who lived with her family in the cottage next to the railway. The house in the background belonged to Henry Murrell and was part of Grange Farm, which extended right through Longacre. The crossing got its name from Windmill Cottages in College Road.

Aug 31   190**5**

To *Mr Gatcum*

❧ **H. MURRELL,** ❧

MARKET GARDENER,

ASH VALE,

ALDERSHOT.

½ lb sholots 2ˢ

Paid Aug 31
J Murrell

Delivered by J Murrell

118. A receipt issued by Henry Murrell of Grange Farm in 1905.

119. An aerial view of Ash Common taken in about 1932. Notice that the field in the foreground, which was called Upper High Field, was still full of crops. At the top right there is a good view of the Ash Hill Recreation Ground, which occupies the site of a former gravel pit, and was bought by the Ash Parish Council in 1895.

120. Grove Road looking towards the *Standard of England* public house in the Ash Hill Road. Heading down the road is Daddy Brooke's pony and cart. Mr. Brooke had a bakery opposite Heathcote School. He had a round red face and was always laughing, and after school boys used to cluster round his delivery van, knowing that they would be offered a bun each.

121. An advertisement for Mr. Brooke's bakery in 1909. Mr. Brooke can be seen in plate 58.

R. BROOKE,

Baker and Confectioner,

ASH COMMON:

Genuine Home-made and Whole-meal Digestive Bread.
Wedding, Luncheon and School Cakes to order.
FAMILIES WAITED UPON DAILY.

122. Grove Villas in Grove Road, where there is still a notice painted on the side advertising 'W. J. Woodman Builder & Co.'. When Mr. Woodman built these houses they cost £250 a pair.

123. An advertisement for Kercher's market garden in 1909.

124. The Bates were also in Grove Road in 1909.

125. Looking up the Ash Hill Road, *c*.1906. The *Bridge House* opened in about 1860, and was a favourite venue for gipsy weddings and funerals. Next door was William Instone's smithy, and his name can just be deciphered on the gates. In the background can be seen the pub sign of the *Standard of England*, and the Ash Jubilee Stores.

126. This advertisement for the Jubilee Stores appeared in St Peter's church magazine in 1909. The stores were in the unusual building at the junction of the Ash Hill Road and Grove Road. By 1925 the Jubilee Stores had become an ironmongery run by Leonard R. Wild. Mr. Wild became well known in Ash because he drove around in a van selling paraffin and other wares.

127. Next door to the Jubilee Stores was the high class grocery run by the Burden family, whose advertisement dates from 1925.

128.   This picture of the crossroads at Wharf Road was taken during the exceptionally hard winter of 1947, when hard-packed ice lay on the road for months. Tank traps from the recent war are still lying at the side of the road. Barlow's Fish and Chip shop can be seen on the corner of Shawfield Road, and part of Tom Bunker's name is visible on the side of the bakery.

129.   This advertisement for A. C. Lloyd is from 1925, by which time the bakery had become the Ash Vale Post Office. It also housed the telephone exchange and boasted the telephone number Ash Vale 1.

ASH VALE BAKERY.

A. C. LLOYD
Baker and Confectioner

Best Wheaten Bread
All kinds of Cakes and Fancies

— • —

Post Office   Ash Vale

E. PIERCY, (Late A. MEABY),
· · · ASH VALE BAKERY, ASH.

French and Dinner Rolls.   Wedding, School and Birthday Cakes.

FAMILIES WAITED UPON DAILY
BEST HOUSEHOLD & WHOLE-MEAL BREAD

130.   The Ash Vale Bakery has had many changes of ownership. Edward Piercy's advertisement dates from 1909.

131. Tom Bunker was baker and postmaster in the
1940s. He is one of the Ash Wardens in plate 113.

Phone: ASH VALE 3201

T. C. BUNKER
and SONS LTD.

Bakers & Confectioners

WEDDING
and
BIRTHDAY
CAKES A
SPECIALITY

POST OFFICE and BAKERY
ASH VALE

132. Next to the bakery was the butchery run by Frederick Charles Hawkins, famed for its sausages. The advertisement
dates from 1909. His son Sydney, who was partially sighted, ran the business after him and started the Ash Blind Club.

F. C. HAWKINS,

Home and Colonial Butcher
ASH VALE.

Best Quality Home-killed Beef, Mutton, Pork
and Veal.

American Chilled Beef and Canterbury Mutton.

Our PORK SAUSAGES a Speciality.

PICKLED TONGUE.

CORNED BEEF

Families supplied at the Lowest Prices, and waited upon daily in all parts of the neighbourhood.

—— *A Trial Solicited.* ——

133. Tolley's shop front with the first proprietor in the doorway, and a quaint old petrol pump outside. The business was established in 1923, and R. F. Tolley went on to be Chairman of the Ash Parish Council for a number of years. The young man in the picture was the firm's first apprentice, Les Storror. Bicycles could be hired for between 2d. and 6d. per hour.

134. Tolley's Garage *c*.1960, with the new premises visible behind the original house. Tolley's Garage is in Ash Hill Road.

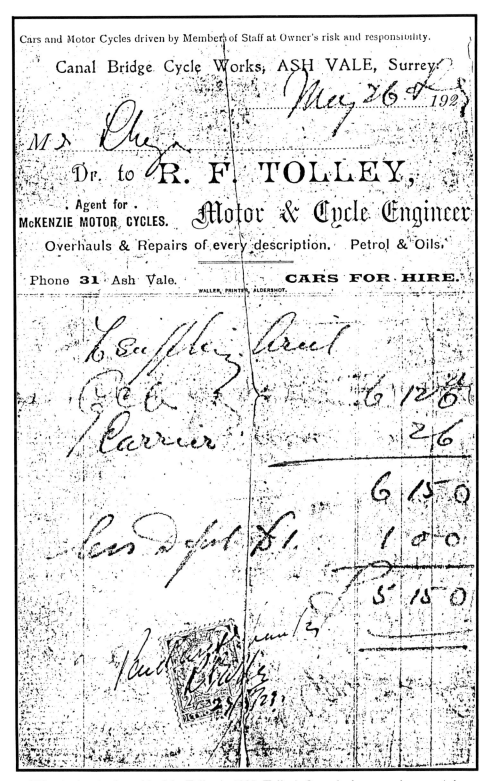

Cars and Motor Cycles driven by Members of Staff at Owner's risk and responsibility.

Canal Bridge Cycle Works, ASH VALE, Surrey.

May 26th 192*7*

M*r* *Chin*

Dr. to R. F. TOLLEY,

. Agent for .
McKENZIE MOTOR CYCLES.

Motor & Cycle Engineer

Overhauls & Repairs of every description. Petrol & Oils.

Phone **31** Ash Vale.

WALLER, PRINTER, ALDERSHOT.

CARS FOR HIRE.

135. An invoice issued by Mr. Tolley in 1927. Tolley's first telephone number was Ash Vale 31.

Established 30 years

TOLLEY'S GARAGE

(R. F. TOLLEY)

 ASH VALE

Phone 2231

The Best Equipped Garage in the Parish

CARS

Agents for STANDARD AND TRIUMPH

CYCLES

Agents for -   -   RALEIGH AND B.S.A.

Welding, High Pressure Greasing and Complete Overhauls a Speciality

136.   This advertisement dates from about 1950.

137. The *Standard of England* in the Ash Hill Road, when the beer was brewed by Harris & Co. of Staines. The picture must have been taken shortly before the pub was sold to Watney, Coombe Reid & Co., *c.*1903. The gentleman perched on the pub sign for a bet, and managed to get down safely.

138. The Methodist church in Wharf Road, which was built in 1878. Every year the children of the Sunday School went on a boat trip along the canal to Frimley.

139.   Wharf Road was very different when this picture was taken. On the right is Balmoral Cottage, where Budgens supermarket is now. Osgood Cottages are still standing, and next to them was the pub called the *George and Dragon*. This was opened by John Woolard, who also owned the next six cottages and some around the corner, in what was to become Woolards Road. The *George and Dragon* closed *c*.1906.

140.   Balmoral Cottage was the home of William Finch, and Mrs. Finch is the lady in front of the house. She died in 1922 aged 93 and her great-niece, Mrs. Blundell, lived in the house until it was demolished to make way for Budgens. Standing at the gate is Mr. Charles Knowles, and standing outside the cottage at the rear of the building is one of the two teachers from Heathcote School to whom it was let.

141. Charles Knowles' boathouse was on Ash Wharf. Mr. Knowles died in 1907 and his wife continued to run the business. In the photograph Mrs. Knowles is the lady standing, and with her is her son. The sign saying 'Boats to let' can just be deciphered on the front of the building. They cost between 6d. and 1s. 6d. per hour, and some were out all day, going as far as Frimley Lock and back.

142. Mrs. Knowles' grandson outside the boathouse, with some of the swans on the canal. Canal cottages are on the opposite bank.

143. The crossroads at Ash Wharf, looking down Shawfield Road, in 1908. Brinkworth's Stores are on the right and Hillary's Stores on the left. At this time Mr. Brinkworth's shop was also the Ash Vale Post Office. Later, the Post Office moved to the Ash Vale Bakery.

144. William Brinkworth was appointed postmaster at Ash Vale in 1898. He was also one of the original trustees of the Victoria Hall in 1897. His advertisement appeared in St Peter's parish magazine in 1909.

POST  OFFICE.

BRINKWORTH'S STORES,

ASH VALE.

Best House for Groceries, Provisions, and all Household Requisites
RELIABLE GOODS ONLY.

☞ *Specialities in CHOICE TEAS AND SELECTED PROVISIONS*

Lowest Possible Prices consistent with Good Quality.   Corn, Meal, and all kinds of Poultry and other Foods.

HILLARY'S POPULAR STORES

Drapers, Milliners, Outfitters,
Boot and Shoe Warehouse.

CARPETS, FLOORCLOTHS.   ✳ ✳   BESPOKE TAILORING

TOYS AND FANCY GOODS.   BIRTHDAY CARDS AND POST CARDS.

Daily Papers, Periodicals & Books supplied promptly and regularly

New and Second-Hand Furniture bought or sold.

Opposite the Post Office, ASH VALE.

145. This advertisement for Hillary's Stores dates from 1909. Arthur Hillary was very well known, particularly for his furniture dealing. He can be seen in the Special Constabulary in plate 42 and he was also one of the wardens shown in plate 113. Mr. W. G. Knott took over from Mr. Hillary and sold toys and clothes, and then Tolley's bought the shop and sold prams, toys and bicycles there.

146.   Shawfield House *c*.1920, when Thomas Osgood was selling it along with Shawfield Farm. Shawfield House was the older building, already there in 1844 when Shawfield was still an area of common stretching west of the present Shawfield Road. Thomas Osgood can be seen in plate 58.

147.   Shawfield Farm, residence of Thomas Osgood, Chairman of the Parish Council, *c*.1920. Both Shawfield Farm and the recreation ground were on land which used to be part of Shawfield. By 1950 this building had become Wychwood School, a boarding and day school run by Miss Yorke Batley. The children of Kim Philby, the spy, were amongst those taught here.

ASH :: SURREY

About 3 miles from the Towns of Aldershot and Farnham.

The Particulars, Plan, and Conditions of Sale

OF

VALUABLE FREEHOLD
RESIDENTIAL PROPERTIES

AT SHAWFIELDS:

SHAWFIELD FARM HOUSE and excellent Garden, with possession on completion.

SHAWFIELD FARM of about $14\frac{1}{4}$ Acres, Farm Buildings, and 2 Cottages, principally with possession.

BUNGALOW COTTAGE and large Garden, in the occupation of Mr. Steeds.

SHAWFIELD HOUSE and Grounds of $3\frac{3}{4}$ Acres.

AT ASH VALE:

BUNGALOW COTTAGE, Garden and Orchard, of $2\frac{3}{4}$ Acres, in the occupation of Mrs. Bond, with possession of the Garden and Orchard.

FOR SALE BY AUCTION BY

MESSRS. HEWETT & LEE

AT

THE LION COUNTY HOTEL, GUILDFORD,

On Tuesday, October 12th, 1920,

at 3 o'clock precisely, in 5 Lots, by instructions from the Owner.

Particulars, Plan, and Conditions of Sale may be obtained of Messrs. FOSTER, WELLS & COGGINS, Solicitors, Aldershot ; or of Messrs. HEWETT & LEE, Chartered Surveyors and Auctioneers, 144 High Street, Guildford, and 65 Chancery Lane, W.C.

BIDDLES LTD., PRINTERS, GUILDFORD.

148.   Sale particulars for Shawfields (*recte* Shawfield) House and Farm, 12 October 1920.

149.   Shawfield United Football Team on the recreation ground in front of Shawfield Farm House. *Standing*: Mr. Taylor is in the middle and Mr. Rogers is on the right. *Middle row*: Mr. Thompson is on the right. *Front row*: Mr. Moore is in the middle. The other players have unfortunately not been identified.

150.   The building on the right, formerly a grocer's shop called the Cambridge Stores, is now a motorbike shop on the Vale Road near the canal bridge. It used to be the *Duke of Cambridge*, which opened in 1857 on what had been part of Ash Common. One of the landlords was George Harris, father of Mrs. Knowles of the boathouse. The pub closed in 1907 and became known as Cambridge House. This picture was taken in the 1950s.

151.   J. Ryan's newsagent's shop in Vale Road in June 1937. The newspaper headlines refer to Jean Harlow, the Hollywood actress, and to Herbert Stanley Morrison, Baron of Lambeth, a well known politician. The shop became the Cabin and was demolished in 1987. Before the Ryans had the shop, it belonged to Miss Hawkins, who sold knitted garments and tapestry work which she made herself. The *Admiral Napier* public house sign is just visible further down the road.

152. Cooper's Stores in the Vale Road, more recently an off-licence. Hereford House can be seen in the background.

T. COOPER

GROCERY & GENERAL STORES

Ash Vale Road

- - - - -

Noted for Mild Cured Bacon.

COOKED MEATS	PATENT MEDICINES
POULTRY FOODS	CONFECTIONERY
GARDEN SEEDS	CIGARETTES
TOBACCO	

153. This advertisement for Cooper's Stores dates from 1925.

154. Hereford House, on the junction between Firacre Road and Vale Road. James Payne built the house, and later Miss Winifred Massey lived there with two aunts, one of whom was Miss Payne of the Post Office at Ash Vale station. After Miss Massey died the proceeds of the sale of the house were divided between two charities, Dr. Barnardo's and the James Payne Memorial Fund.

155. Miss Massey ran a school at Hereford House, to which children were sent for 2s. 6d. a week. Many other local children attended solely for music lessons. This is an advertisement for Miss Massey's school in 1925.

Miss Winifred C. Massey

Receives   L.V.C.M.

Pupils for Pianoforte and Violin

also for

Painting in Oils, Watercolours, Pen-painting, etc.

Portraits and Pictures executed
:: in Oils and Watercolours ::

HEREFORD HOUSE, ASH VALE

Corner of Firacre Road

156. St Mary's church at Ash Vale. The original iron church on the left of the picture was erected in 1885, and cost £205. It soon became too small, so the present church was built in 1906 by W. J. Woodman at a cost of £864, the bricks being brought on the canal and unloaded at Ash Wharf. The old iron church became the church hall, until it was finally replaced by the new community centre in 1979.

157. This cottage was one of four small buildings which formed the glue factory which was opened near Firacre House *c.*1864. Glue for postage stamps was produced, and also the glaze for picture postcards and playing cards. The factory closed in 1924.

158. The canal and the backs of some of the houses in Hutton Road, *c.*1906. Further along the canal was Springfield, which has now become a housing estate. Annual fetes were held there by St Peter's church in conjunction with St Mary's. These always ended with a greasy pole contest across the canal.

159. Richard Bateman, *c.*1910, the nephew of William Bateman in plate 74. He was married at St Peter's church in 1877, lived at Foxhurst in Ash Vale, and was a churchwarden at St Peter's church from 1902 to 1913, where there is a brass plaque erected in his memory.

160. Foxhurst *c.*1905, the home of Richard Bateman's family. Foxhurst was in Prospect Road, and was known in later years for the model railway in the garden. The house was demolished to make way for Foxhurst Road.

161. A similar fate befell Gorselands, a large house which was built around 1907 where Gorselands Close is now.

Elleray Private Hotel

ASH VALE.

♣ ♣ ♣

Charming Situation.
Newly Furnished and Decorated
Dance Floor.
'Four acres of Garden to Canal
Garages
Aldershot 10 minutes

♣ ♣ ♣

Applications: Manageress, "Elleray,"
Prospect Road, Ash Vale.

Phone –Ash Vale 79

162. Elleray was a big house in Prospect Road which became an hotel before it was replaced by the Elleray Court flats. This advertisement dates from 1925.

163. The *Swan* (Heathvale Bridge Road), *c*.1902. John Tupper opened the pub, a free house, *c*.1857, and it is still known locally as *Tupper's Tavern*. Customers included Charles Kingsley, and the famous prize fighters Tom Sayers and John Heenan. The pub contained a rat pit, and there was cockfighting and pigeon shooting. Edward Tupper was the next landlord, and in his time there were dances on the lawn in summer while the Salvation Army band played, and customers amused themselves in a large maze.

164. This advertisement for *Tupper's* dates from 1911. *Tupper's Tavern* was so popular with the army that its name was known throughout the world.

TUPPER'S (SWAN HOTEL). TELE. 92 NORTH CAMP.
ASH RANGES. ASH VALE,
WINES, SPIRITS & BEERS of the Finest Quality.

Luncheons, Teas, and Dinners on the Shortest Notice   Catering for Large or Small Parties
Accommodation for Cyclists & Tourists.   Fine Tea Lawn and Bowling Green now opened.
Mr. Rowllings' String Orchestra plays selections of music on the Bowling Green every
Wednesday from 7 till 9.30 p.m

165. Heath Vale Bridge, commonly known as Tupper's Bridge, and the back of *Tupper's*, in 1905. Many parties and couples arrived at the pub by boat.

166. Steel Hill had very few trees when this picture was taken. The hill is behind the St John's Ambulance Headquarters in Heathvale Bridge Road.

167. View along the Basingstoke Canal looking towards the railway bridge near Ash Vale station. Harmsworth's boathouse is on the left, and his boat building yard is on the opposite bank. Alexander John Harmsworth, the eldest son of a carpenter working on the canal, was brought up in Ash. After marrying he lived on a house-boat at Ash Vale, and gradually built up the pleasure boat business evident in the photograph. He bought the canal with all its wharves and cottages in 1923.

168. Harmsworth started buying barges in 1902. This one was called *Dauntless*. During the First World War German prisoners of war like these were put to work on the canal, carrying out maintenance and unloading. In 1918 Harmsworth began to build his own barges and local people, especially children, enjoyed watching the work.

169. The view from Harmsworth's boathouse, looking south along the canal. In the 1920s and 1930s canoes, punts and rowing boats could be hired for 1s. 6d. an hour.

170. The view north along the canal from the Ash Vale railway bridge. Alexander Harmsworth's brother used to run a shop selling fishing tackle one hundred yards along the towpath. If they could afford it, local children used to buy real hooks and floats there, to replace their home-made ones.

171. The canal cottage in this picture is thought to be Mr. Harmsworth's shop, but there were a number of similar canal cottages in Ash Vale.

172. The original Ash Vale station building, opened on 2 May 1870 by the London and South Western Railway Company. It was called North Camp and Ash Vale until 1924, and the Victorian buildings survived until 1974. In the 1890s rambling roses were grown by the stationmaster, Charles Hatcher, along the whole length of both platforms. At the top of the road is the entrance to Harmsworth's boat building yard.

173.   The railway bridge at Ash Vale station. The building on the right was the Ash Vale Station Post Office run by Miss Edith Payne. William Newton, whose cycle shop is on the left, later took over the Post Office building, now the premises of Parkers Estate Agency, and sold motorbikes. His son, Nipper Newton, became a famous motorcyclist and rode for England in 1938. The other shop on the left was Bridgstock's Grocery and Provision Stores.

174.   A 1925 advertisement for Bridgstock's shop.

THE RAILWAY

Grocery and Provision Stores

ASH VALE

Finest Danish Breakfast Bacon
Golden Meadow Fresh Butter
Jams   Marmalades   Biscuits
·::   All Best Makes   ::

Families waited upon Daily.   A Trial Order solicited

F. BRIDGSTOCK

175. Lysons Avenue at the beginning of the century, with the rows of poplars along each side which were pollarded in 1915. The local boys used to have a cricket pitch amongst the heather and gorse on the common land next to the road. The common has now become an industrial area and the trees are all gone.

176. Looking towards Mytchett from the bridge at Ash Vale station. The house in the centre of the picture, Valecroft, was the home of Samuel Cody. He became the first man to fly in Great Britain in 1908 and worked on 'man-lifting kites' for the Army. Cody was killed in 1913 when his aircraft crashed.

177. Samuel Cody's funeral, just leaving Valecroft. His funeral, with full military honours, started from his home and made its way to the Aldershot Military Cemetery. It was described by a local resident as 'the greatest affair Ash Vale ever saw', with the four massed bands and the gun carriage.

178. The V.E. celebrations at Prospect Farm in Ash Vale. The party took place in a large field alongside Prospect Road, north of the farm buildings. The farm became the Prospect Country Club in 1961, and the gentleman lying in the grass holding the calf is Mr. Richards, the owner. The farm's prize stud boar was the star of the event. He was unusually tame and could be safely led along in carnival processions and allowed near to children.